SKILLS FOR LITERACY

Book 1

Geoff Frohlich

Curriculum Concepts
comprehensive coverage

Skills for Literacy

ISBN 9781906125233

Ordering Code – UK0341

Curriculum Concepts UK

The Old School

Upper High Street

Bedlinog

Mid-Glamorgan CF46 6SA

Email: orders@curriculumconcepts.co.uk

www.curriculumconcepts.co.uk

Copyright © Geoff Frohlich

First published in United Kingdom, 2007

Revised and published Curriculum Concepts New Zealand, 2006

Copyright Information

This master may only be reproduced by the original purchaser for use with their class(es) only. The publisher prohibits the loaning or on selling of this master for the purpose of reproduction.

Illustrated by Karla Vink

Y1 - T1, WL 3, 4, 5
    Rhyming families
        ing 36
        ay 37
    Hearing initial and final phonemes in CVC words
        ig, an, en, ot, ug 38
        at, et, in, op, un 39
        ap, eb, ib, og, ow, ud, ed, id, up, ad, ut, am 40
    Revision - rhyming families word search
        and, in, en, ut 41
        ot, et, an, un 42
    Revision - complete words in a sentence - ad, an, at, - ot, et, ake - ig, in, it 43

Y1 - T2, WL 2
    Alphabetical order
        introduction 44
        basic words / classroom words 45
        general - looking at the second letter 46
        fruit 47
        animals 48
        letters and words 49
        letters and words 50
        make a sentence 51
        make a pattern 52

Sentence level work - sentence construction and punctuation
Y1 - T1, SL 5, 6, 7, 8, 9
    Full stops and capital letters 53
    Full stops and capital letters 54
    Capital
        S 55
        M 56
        H 57
        F 58
        B 59
        W 60
        P 61
        C 62

Contents

Teacher Notes iii

Word level work - Phonics
RY WL 2a, b, c, d
Y1 - T1, WL 2
    Initial phoneme (sounds)
        b 1
        c 2
        d 3
        f 4
        g 5
        h 6
        j 7
        k 8
        l 9
        m 10
        n 11
        p 12
        qu 13
        r 14
        s 15
        t 16
        v 17
        w 18
        x y z 19
    Revision
        s, m, h, f 20
        b, w, p, c 21
        m, s, p, c 22
        d l, g, j 23
        n, r, y k 24

RY, WL, 2c, d
    Digraphs
        th 25
        th 26
        sh 27
        sh 28
        ch 29
        ch 30

RY, WL, R2 e (4a)
Y1 - T1, WL 1a, b
Y2 - T2 WL 1
    Identify families of rhyming CVC words
        ig, ad, in, et, en, un, an, ot, ar, ay, at, it 31
        am, in, ut, ob, it, aw, op, ip, eg, ed, ag, ap 32
        ad, an, at 33
        ot, et, ug 34
        ig, in, it 35

Teacher Notes

Series Coverage

There are four books in the *Skills for Literacy* series. The activities in each book work progressively through the skills and knowledge that are required from Reception through to Year 2 Term 3.

Book 1   Reception Year, Year 1 – Term 1 requirements plus some Year 1 – Term 2
Book 2   Year 1 – Term 3
Book 3   Year 1 – Term 3
Book 4   Year 2 – Term 1, Term 2, Term 3

How to use the activities in this book

The activities can be used as A4, A3 or A5 size depending on the way they are to be used with students. These activities are ideal to assist with the introduction of the skills to students as part of the Literacy Hour or as independent work.

Teacher instruction –

Shared class or group work

- Enlarge as a chart or show on white board.

Independent work – shared group

- Enlarge as a chart so students can all see and contribute.

Independent work– individual

- give out as A4 sheet so students can complete it independently. It is very important that after students have completed the activity they read it to themselves and/or to a friend and they take it home to read to their family. The worksheets can be kept in a folder or be made into a book so students can reread them and reinforce the vocabulary and skills covered.

Curriculum Links

The activities in this book are organised into either **Word level work** related to **phonics, spelling** and **vocabulary** or **Sentence level work** related to **grammar** and **sentence construction** and **punctuation** for Reception Year, Year 1 - Term 1 and Year 1 - Term 2.

The specific objectives from **National Literacy Strategy** that are covered by the activities in this book are listed on the next page. (Note: This is not all the objectives for each year, just those covered). The objectives have been numbered as per the document and additional identifiers eg a, b, c added for easy reference. This reference (2a) along with the year and type of work is shown on the contents page so that teachers can see at a glance which activities relate to which objectives.

Eg (RY, WL 2a = Reception Year, Word Level, Objective 2a).

The alphabet letter/sound activities are organised in alphabetical order so that teachers can easily locate the letter/sound they want to reinforce in the order they want to introduce them.

National Literacy Strategy links

Reception Year   RY

WL - Word level work: Phonological awareness, phonics and spelling

Pupils should be taught:

2. knowledge of grapheme/phoneme correspondences through:
   a. hearing and identifying initial sounds in words;
   b. reading letters(s) that represent(s) the sound(s); a-z, ch, sh, th;
   c. writing each letter in response to each sound: a-z, ch, sh, th;
   d. identifying and writing initial and dominant phonemes in spoken words;
   e. identifying and writing initial and final phonemes in consonant-vowel-consonant (CVC) words, e.g. fit, mat, pan;
4. to link sound and spelling patterns by:
   a. using knowledge of rhyme to identify families of rhyming CVC words, e.g. *hop, top, mop; fat, mat, pat,* etc.

Year 1 - Term 1   Y1-T1

WL - Word level work: Phonological awareness, phonics and spelling

Pupils should be taught:

1. from YR, to practise and secure the ability to rhyme, and to relate this to spelling patterns through:
   a. exploring and playing with rhyming patterns;
   b. generating rhyming strings, e.g. fat, hat, pat;
2. from YR, to practise and secure alphabetic letter knowledge and alphabetic order;
3. from YR to practrise and secure the ability to hear initial and final phonemes in CVC words, e.g. fit, mat, pan;
4. to discriminate and segment all three phonemes in CVC words;
5. to blend phonemes to read CVC words in rhyming and non-rhyming sets;

SL - Sentence level work: Sentence construction and punctuation

5. to recognise full stops and capital letters when reading, and name them correctly;
6. to begin using the term sentence to identify sentences in text;
7. that a line of writing is not necessasrily the same as a sentence;
8. to begin using full stops to demarcate sentences;
9. to use a capital letter for the personal pronoun 'I' and for the start of a sentence.

Year 1 - Term 2   Y1-T2

WL - Word level work: Phonological awareness, phonics and spelling

1. to secure identification, spelling and reading of initial, final and medial letter sounds in simple words; vowels.

Name [ ] [ ] **b**

Put in the letter b to make the word.

Look at the ☐ell.

Look at the ☐all.

Look at the ☐ear.

Look at the ☐ird.

This is a ☐ike.

This is a ☐oat.

This is a ☐anana.

This is a ☐aby.

👀 **Read each sentence.**

Read the words beginning with b.

be	bit	ball	boy
by	bat	boat	baby
big	bed	been	but

Name ☐ | c

Put in the letter c to make the word.

Look at the ☐at.

Look at the ☐ow.

Look at the ☐ar.

Look at the ☐ake.

This is a ☐astle.

This is a ☐up.

This is a ☐arrot.

This is a ☐amera.

👁 👁 **Read each sentence.**

Read the words beginning with c.

cat	can	come	coat
cow	call	came	could
cup	cut	carrot	can't

Name [ ] [ ] d

Put in the letter d to make the word.

Look at the ⬜og.

Look at the ⬜olphin.

Look at the ⬜uck.

Look at the ⬜eer.

This is a ⬜esk.

This is a ⬜oughnut.

This is a ⬜inosaur.

This is a ⬜onkey.

👀 **Read each sentence.**

Read the words beginning with d.

day	dad	dig	down
dog	did	do	door
dot	don't	dam	duck

© Curriculum Concepts   Skills for Literacy – Book 1   3

Name [   ] ☐ f

Put in the letter f to make the word.

Look at the ☐ire.

Look at the ☐ish.

Look at the ☐ire-engine.

Look at the ☐an.

This is a ☐ork.

This is a ☐inger.

This is a ☐ence.

This is a ☐eather.

👀 **Read each sentence.**

Read the words beginning with f.

for	fit	fin	fire
fun	food	fan	feet
fat	face	first	four

Name [ ] g

Put in the letter g to make the word.

Look at the ☐eyser.

Look at the ☐oat.

Look at the ☐uitar.

Look at the ☐irl.

This is a ☐ate.

This is a ☐olfclub.

This is a ☐arden.

This is a ☐orilla.

👀 **Read each sentence.**

Read the words beginning with g.

go	gap	girl	gone
got	goes	goat	give
get	good	going	gold

Name [ ] ☐ **h**

Put in the letter h to make the word.

Look at the ☐ouse.
Look at the ☐elicopter.
Look at the ☐ammer.
Look at the ☐orse.
This is a ☐eart.
This is a ☐at.
This is a ☐orn.
This is a ☐hand.

 Read each sentence.

Read the words beginning with h.

he	hat	house	hand
has	had	her	here
home	hit	have	help

Name [   ] [ ] j

Put in the letter j to make the word.

Look at the ☐et.

Look at the ☐ellyfish.

Look at the ☐ack.

Look at the ☐ack-in-the-box.

This is a milk ☐ug.

This is a ☐igsaw.

This is a ☐ar.

This is a ☐acket.

👁👁 **Read each sentence.**

Read the words beginning with j.

jug	jog	jet	jump
jam	jot	June	jumped
jar	Jack	just	January

© Curriculum Concepts — Skills for Literacy – Book 1 — 7

Name ☐ **k**

Put in the letter k to make the word.

Look at the ☐ing.

Look at the ☐ey.

Look at the ☐ite.

Look at the ☐ettle.

This is a ☐iwi.

This is a ☐angeroo.

This is a ☐itten.

This is a ☐ingfisher.

👀 **Read each sentence.**

Read the words beginning with l.

king	keen	key	kerb
keep	kill	kite	kick
kid	kind	kiss	kitten

8   Skills for Literacy – Book 1   © Curriculum Concepts

Name [   ]   [ ] l

Put in the letter l to make the word.

Look at the ☐ion.

Look at the ☐amb.

Look at the ☐etterbox.

Look at the ☐obster.

This is a ☐ollipop.

This is a ☐eg.

This is a ☐ightbulb.

This is a ☐emon.

👁👁 **Read each sentence.**

Read the words beginning with l.

let	log	long	live
lit	leg	last	little
lot	like	look	light

© Curriculum Concepts   Skills for Literacy – Book 1   9

Name ☐ ☐ **m**

Put in the letter m to make the word.

Look at the ☐an.

Look at the ☐ap.

Look at the ☐onkey.

Look at the ☐otorcycle.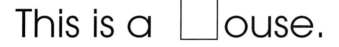

This is a ☐ushroom.

This is a ☐ouse.

This is a ☐ountain.

This is a ☐atch.

👁👁 **Read each sentence.**

Read the words beginning with m.

me	mum	mud	more
my	mat	make	must
may	made	man	many

10   Skills for Literacy – Book 1   © Curriculum Concepts

Name ☐ ☐ n

Put in the letter n to make the word.

Look at the ☐urse.

Look at the ☐est.

Look at the fish in the ☐et.

The ☐appy is on the baby.

This is a ☐ut.

This is a ☐eedle.

This is a ☐ewspaper.

This is the number ☐ine.

👁👁 **Read each sentence.**

Read the words beginning with n.

no	new	nine	next
net	nap	nail	night
nut	now	not	name

Name ☐

Put in the letter p to make the word.

Look at the ☐ig.

Look at the ☐oliceman.

Look at the ☐ainter.

Look at the ☐irate.

This is a ☐anda.

This is a ☐ie.

This is a ☐encil.

This is a ☐ear.

 **Read each sentence.**

Read the words beginning with p.

pat	pan	pet	pull
pie	pen	pin	push
pig	put	pink	people

12 Skills for Literacy – Book 1 © Curriculum Concepts

Name [ ] [ ] **qu**

When a word begins with **q,** it always has a **u** after it.

Put in the letters qu to make the word.

Look at the [ ]een.

Look at my [ ]ilt.

Look at the [ ]ail.

This is a [ ]estion mark. **?**

This is a [ ]arter.

This is a [ ]aver.

A [ ]estion mark goes at the end of a [ ]estion.

👀 **Read each sentence.**

Read the words beginning with qu.

queen   quilt   quail

question   quaver   quarter

quick   quiet   quid

© Curriculum Concepts   Skills for Literacy – Book 1

Name ☐ ☐ **r**

Put in the letter r to make the word.

This is my ☐abbit.

Look at the ☐hinoceros.

Look at the ☐ocket.

This is a big ☐at.

This is a ☐uler.

This is a ☐ake?

Look at my new ☐adio.

Look at the ☐ooster.

Read each sentence.

Read the words beginning with r.

rat	run	ring	rabbit
rag	ran	rake	right
rug	rib	rest	round
red	ram	ride	road

Skills for Literacy – Book 1 © Curriculum Concepts

Name ☐ | S |

Put in the letter s to make the word.

Look at the ☐ nail.
Look at the ☐ ack.
Look at the ☐ ail.
Look at the ☐ eal.
This is a ☐ ock.
This is a ☐ andwich.
This is a ☐ ausage.
This is a ☐ aw.

👀 **Read each sentence.**

Read the words beginning with s.

so	set	sing	saw
see	sat	sink	seen
sit	sun	some	said

Name [   ] [ ] t

Put in the letter t to make the word.

Look at the ☐unnel.

Look at the ☐v.

Look at the ☐iger.

Look at the ☐urtle.

This is a ☐ape.

This is a ☐elephone.

This is a ☐able.

This is a ☐oothbrush.

  Read each sentence.

Read the words beginning with t.

to	tap	tan	top
took	tip	ten	tall
take	top	tin	today

Name [   ]

Put in the letter v to make the word.

Look at the ☐ase.

Look at the ☐ideo.

Look at the ☐iolin.

Look at the ☐egetables.

This is a ☐an.

This is a ☐olcano.

This is a ☐ulture.

This is a ☐et.

  Read each sentence.

Read the words beginning with v.

| vase | van | vowel |
| vet | very | violet |

© Curriculum Concepts   Skills for Literacy – Book 1

Name ▢ W

Put in the letter w to make the word.

Look at the ▢olf.

Look at my ▢atch.

Look at the ▢indmill.

Look at the ▢itch.

This is a ▢indow.

This is a ▢eb.

This is ▢atermelon.

This is a ▢asp.

👀 **Read each sentence.**

Read the words beginning with w.

we	well	want	water
went	will	win	with
were	was	walk	way

Name ☐ | x y z

Put in the letter to make the word.

Look at the ☐-ray.

Look at the ☐acht.

Look at the ☐ebra.

The ☐ebra is in the ☐oo.

This is a ☐yloplone.

This is a ☐oyo.

This is a ☐ip.

This is a ☐ig ☐ag.

👁👁 **Read each sentence.**

Read the words beginning with x y z

xylophone   x-ray

you   yes   your   year

zip   zoo   zebra

Name [ ]   s m h f

Put in the letter to make the word.

This is a ☐and.

This is a ☐addle.

I like the ☐onkey.

This is a ☐ish.

This is a ☐ish-hook.

This is a ☐otorcycle.

I like the ☐orse.

I like the ☐unhat.

  Read each sentence.

Read the words. Match to the pictures.

bell   hammer

sock   pirate

finger   mushroom

cake   window

Name [   ] **b w p c**

Put in the letter to make the word.

This is a ☐atch.

Look at the ☐aby.

This is a ☐ig.

Look at the ☐at.

This is a ☐anda.

Look at the ☐arrot.

This is a ☐ike.

Look at the ☐asp.

👀 **Read each sentence.**

Read the words. Match to the pictures.

ball		heart
sack		piano
mouse		feather
cow	 	windmill

© Curriculum Concepts — Skills for Literacy – Book 1 — 21

Name [ ] m s p c

Put in the letter to make the word.

Look at the ☐ar.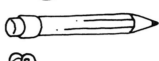

This is a ☐encil.

Look at the ☐ouse.

This is a ☐aw.

Look at the ☐amera.

This is a ☐eal.

Look at the ☐an.

This is a ☐irate.

  Read each sentence.

Read the words. Match to the picture.

fish

banana

cup

soap

monkey

pig

witch

helicopter

22   Skills for Literacy – Book 1   © Curriculum Concepts

Name [ ] | d l g j |

Put in the letter to make the word.

Look at the ☐ion.

Here is a ☐ift for you.

This is a ☐iger.

Look at the ☐ug.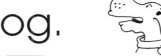

Here is a ☐og.

Look at the ☐uitar.

Here is a ☐ellyfish.

  Read each sentence.

Read the words. Match to the pictures.

torch  kangaroo

jet  lollipop

nest rainbow

deer   goat

© Curriculum Concepts — Skills for Literacy – Book 1

Name [   ] | n r y k |

Put in the letter to make the word.

Look at the ☐nest.

This is a ☐ug.

I like my ☐ite.

This is a ☐ey.

Look at the ☐acht.

I like the ☐ecklace.

Look at the ☐abbit.

This is the ☐oke of the egg.

  Read each sentence.

Read the words. Match to the pictures.

nine   yacht

zebra     quail

gate   lollipop

rake    king

24   Skills for Literacy – Book 1   © Curriculum Concepts

Name ☐

(Circle) **the letters that are the same in all these words.**

the   than   this   that
they   there   those   them
              then

The letters are ☐

Put in the letters. Write the word.

__ __ e   _____   _____

__ __ is   _____   _____

__ __ ey   _____   _____

__ __ at   _____   _____

__ __ an   _____   _____

__ __ en   _____   _____

👁👁 **Read each word.**

Name ☐ ☐ **th**

Put in the letters th to make the word.

☐e ball is red.

Look at ☐at big fish!

"Go ☐ere" said the teacher.

☐en the girls went home.

We waited for ☐em.

☐ey were very nice.

☐ose are my socks.

☐is is ☐e end.

👀 **Read each sentence.**

Circle the words beginning with th.

Pig   look   Mary   look

this   tea   what
       there
that   play   go   they

Name  **sh**

Circle the pictures that begin like

Put in the letters.

I like my ☐oes.

Look at this ☐ell.

Look at my ☐orts.

"This is my pet ☐eep,"

☐e said.

Look at the ☐ark!

 Read each sentence to a friend.

Name [   ]   [ ] **sh**

Put in the letters sh to make the word.

Please [ ]ut the door.

What [ ]ape is this?

I like finding [ ]ells on the sand.

We do not [ ]out inside.

I got new [ ]oes for the party.

A knife is [ ]arp.

A big boat is a [ ]ip.

A [ ]ark has [ ]arp teeth.

👀 **Read each sentence.**

Circle the words beginning with sh.

shy   chop   shop   shot

show   ship   sharp   on

shed   shout   chin   go

28   Skills for Literacy – Book 1   © Curriculum Concepts

Name [   ] [ ] **ch**

Circle the pictures that begin like

  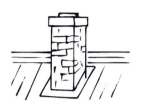 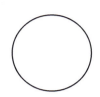

Put in the letters.

This is a ☐ain.

Look at the ☐urch.

I like ☐ocolate.

I like this ☐air.

This is a ☐imney.

This is my ☐in.

 Read the sentences to a friend.

Name ☐ ☐ **ch**

Put in the letters ch to make the word.

A hen is a ☐icken.

A pirate's treasure ☐est is big.

We like ☐eese.

You sit on a ☐air.

You have a ☐in on your face.

I like to ☐op firewood.

We are having fish and ☐ips.

We use ☐alk on a blackboard.

A boy or a girl is a ☐ild.

Smoke goes up the ☐imney.

👀 **Read each sentence.**

Skills for Literacy – Book 1 © Curriculum Concepts

Name ☐

Read and say – cross out the odd word. <u>Underline</u> the letters that are the same in the other words.

1. d<u>ad</u> b<u>ad</u> s<u>ad</u> ~~the~~
2. big pig wig mum
3. the tin win bin
4. get said let net
5. hen pen got ten
6. fun gun van bun
7. man pan big ran
8. hot got lot get
9. dad car far tar
10. day say way do
11. cat bat sat house
12. cut lit bit fit

Name

Read and say – cross out the odd word. <u>Underline</u> the letters that are the same in the other words.

1. h<u>am</u>　d<u>am</u>　~~pop~~　j<u>am</u>
2. leg　bin　pin　tin
3. but　sob　hut　nut
4. pin　sob　job　rob
5. bit　fit　sit　one
6. ten　paw　jaw　saw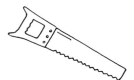
7. top　pop　hop　lip
8. pop　lip　sip　tip
9. beg　out　leg　peg
10. led　bed　red　tan
11. rag　cup　tag　bag
12. map　tap　sad　cap

Name [____] ad, an, at

Make and read the new words.

ad	an	at
b<u>ad</u>	b___	b___
d___	c___	c___
f___	f___	f___
h___	m___	h___
l___	p___	m___
m___	r<u>an</u>	p___
p___	t___	r___
s___	v___	s___
gl___	th___	th<u>at</u>

Circle the word that matches each picture.

Name [_____] ot, et, ug

Make and read the new words.

ot	et	ug
c<u>ot</u>	b___	b___
d___	g___	h___
g___	j___	j___
h___	l___	ch___
l___	m<u>et</u>	m___
n___	n___	r___
p___	p___	sn___
r___	s___	t___
j___	v___	pl<u>ug</u>

Circle the word that matches each picture.

Name ☐ | ig, in, it

Make and read the new words.

ig	in	it
b<u>ig</u>	b____	b____
d____	f____	f____
f____	d____	h____
j____	k____	k____
g____	p<u>in</u>	l____
p____	s____	gr____
r____	t____	p____
tw____	w____	s____
w____	ch____	w<u>it</u>

(Circle) the word that matches each picture.

Skills for Literacy – Book 1

Name _____ | ing |

Make and read the new words.
Make one of your own.

ing

ding	fl_____	k _____
cl_____	p _____	sl_____
r_____	st _____	s _____
sw_____	w _____	th_____
z_____	br_____	str_____
_____	_____	_____

Put in the ing word that makes sense.

I _____ in the choir.

The bird's _____ was hurt.

Can I _____ my sister too?

Name ☐ ☐ **ay**

Put in the letters to complete the word for each day of the week.

Mond____   Tuesd____

Wednesd____   Thursd____

Frid____   Saturd____

Sund____

Read each word. (Circle) day.

Put in the letters to complete the words.

The month of M____.

Go out to pl____.

s____   st____

w____   b____

h____   p____

l____   sw____

Name

Say the word for each picture. Put in the missing letters. Write a word of your own for each rhyming family.

 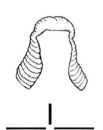 
_i_ _i_ _i_ _i_

_a_ _a_ _a_ _a_

  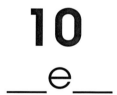
_e_ _e_ _e_ _e_

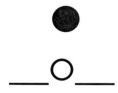 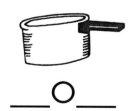 
_o_ _o_ _o_ _o_

_u_ _u_ _u_ _u_

Name

Say the word for each picture. Put in the missing letters. Write a word of your own for each rhyming family.

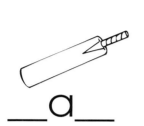 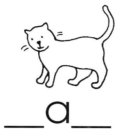 

_a_ _a_ _a_ _a_

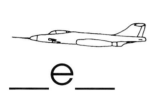  

_e_ _e_ _e_ _e_

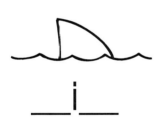  

_i_ _i_ _i_ _i_

_o_ _o_ _o_ _o_

_u_ _u_ _u_ _u_

© Curriculum Concepts   Skills for Literacy – Book 1   39

Name

Say the word for each picture. Put in the missing letters. Write a word that rhymes with each.

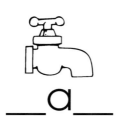 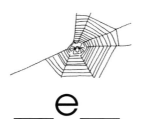  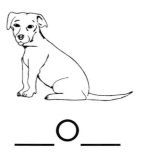

__a__ __e__ _i_ __o__

___   ___   ___   ___

__o__ __u__ __e__ _i_

___   ___   ___   ___

_u_ _a_ _u_ _a_

___   ___   ___   ___

Name

Find the hidden words.

b	a	n	d	t	n	u	t	z	c
f	d	t	q	k	w	y	j	s	a
i	t	b	g	z	x	e	r	a	n
n	f	u	u	e	t	x	b	n	j
y	p	z	t	t	i	n	h	d	f
h	e	n	s	e	r	p	i	n	l
s	n	o	t	l	h	b	z	x	e
x	t	k	r	a	u	i	p	h	l
m	u	e	n	n	t	n	b	a	n
z	r	d	n	d	j	x	h	n	u
n	e	m	n	p	e	t	n	d	g

band	bin	hen	but
hand	fin	men	hut
land	pin	pen	gut
sand	tin	ten	nut

Name

Find the hidden words.

g	o	t	t	e	b	w	x	z	c
f	d	t	q	k	w	y	j	p	a
u	t	o	e	z	x	e	r	h	n
n	f	u	g	e	t	x	b	o	j
y	q	z	k	p	a	n	h	t	f
d	v	w	s	e	r	u	i	o	l
s	l	o	t	i	d	f	z	x	e
x	n	k	r	a	n	i	p	o	t
m	u	z	q	r	s	w	b	v	n
a	r	d	f	g	j	u	h	y	u
n	p	s	n	p	e	t	n	v	g

got   bet   can   fun
hot   get   pan   gun
lot   let   ran   run
pot   pet   man   sun

Name [ ]

Put in ad, an, at to complete the word.

I love my d[ad].

A frying p[an].

I saw B[at]man.

My pussyc[at] is black.

I saw Batm[an].

An angry person is m[ad].

Put in ot, et, ake to complete the word.

A fire is h[ot].

This plane is a j[et].

I like eating c[ake].

This is a r[ake].

Our baby sleeps in a c[ot].

I have a p[et] dog.

Put in ig, in, it to complete the word.

This animal is a p[ig].

Here is a t[in] can.

Do not h[it] other people.

A giant is b[ig].

S[it] on the mat.

Put rubbish in the b[in].

Read each sentence.

Name

When you say the alphabet 'a' is the first letter you say and 'z' is the last. We can put words into the same order as the letters in the alphabet.

The words in the box are in **alphabetical order** –

The first letter of each word is used to put the words in the order of the alphabet.

The first letter of the first word is 'a'. Because 'a' is the first letter of the alphabet, this word comes first.

The first letter of the last word is 'z'. Because 'z' is the last letter of the alphabet, this word comes last.

and
big
cat
dog
zoo

Complete and say the alphabet.

__ b c __ e __ g h __ j __ l __

n __ __ q r s __ __ v w __ __ z

Put these words into alphabetical order. Remember to look at the first letter of each word.

car   do   for   but   and   home

1. _____
2. _____
3. _____
4. _____
5. _____
6. _____

Name

Complete and say the alphabet.

a __ __ d __ f __ __ i __ k __ m __

o p __ __ __ t u __ __ x y __

Put these words into alphabetical order.

go   see   am   was   you

1. _____
2. _____
3. _____
4. _____
5. _____

These things are found in the classroom. Put them in alphabetical order.

desk   ruler   book   chair   pencil

1. _____
2. _____
3. _____
4. _____
5. _____

Name _____

Sometimes you will find no words beginning with the letter 'a', so you then look for the next letter of the alphabet. Not all the alphabet is here, so be careful!

Put these words into alphabetical order.

bell _____

map _____

stop _____

go _____

fast _____

hot _____

cold _____

is _____

not _____

dish _____

zoo _____

they _____

queen _____

read _____

pig _____

Name

Put these names of fruit into alphabetical order.

lemon   _____

orange   _____

apple   _____

pear   _____

watermelon _____

banana   _____

mango   _____

strawberry _____

grapes   _____

coconut   _____

raspberry _____

kiwifruit _____

Complete the alphabet.

a __ __ __ __ __ g __ __ __ k l __ __ o __ __ __ __ __ __ __ __ w __ __ z

Name

Put these names of animals into alphabetical order.

dog
rabbit
lion
alligator
pig
whale
cat
zebra
frog
bear
tiger
elephant
monkey
horse
snail
kangaroo
octopus
grasshopper
unicorn

_____
_____
_____
_____
_____
_____
_____
_____
_____
_____
_____
_____
_____
_____
_____
_____
_____
_____
_____

Name

A. Complete and say the alphabet.

_ b _ _ _ f _ h _ _ _ l m _ _ p _ r _ _ u _ _ x _ _

B. Write each group of letters in alphabetical order.

1. c a z s k _____
2. q t n l w _____
3. y g r b x _____
4. i m d j o _____
5. p h k c e _____
6. b v x c z _____
7. q w e r t _____
8. a s d f g _____

C. Write these words in alphabetical order.

1. fat   sat   mat   pat   _____
2. hit   pit   lit   wit   _____
3. put   but   hut   rut   _____
4. tin   pin   bin   win   _____
5. pet   vet   get   net   _____
6. rub   cub   tub   hub   _____

D. Look at the second letter as well as the first before putting these words in alphabetical order.

too   _____
wig   _____
band _____
but   _____
stamp _____
fist _____
sand _____
get   _____

© Curriculum Concepts   Skills for Literacy – Book 1

Name

A. Complete and say the alphabet.

a b __ d __ f __ h __ __ k l __ n __ p q __ s t __ v w __ __ z

B. Write these letters in alphabetical order.

1. p o i u y _____
2. l k j h g _____
3. m n b v c _____
4. y h n j u _____
5. y h n b g _____
6. c d e r t _____
7. z x s a q _____
8. u j m n h _____

C. Write these letters in alphabetical order.

1. leg   peg   beg   keg   _____
2. bun   run   fun   sun   _____
3. pen   ten   hen   den   _____
4. rug   tug   mug   bug   _____
5. hot   lot   rot   cot   _____
6. job   Bob   sob   rob   _____

D. Look at the second letter as well as the first before putting these words in alphabetical order.

toy _____

went _____

wand _____

tent _____

stop _____

frog _____

funny _____

get _____

Name

Put the words into alphabetical order to make a sentence.

1. painting today I'm
   _____

2. lollies I like
   _____

3. well can read I
   _____

4. Toni home said Go
   _____

5. people work Buses to carry
   _____

6. I home to At yell like
   _____

Look at the second letter, as well as the first before putting these words in alphabetical order.

zoo   _____

pig   _____

land   _____

put   _____

story   _____

list   _____

said   _____

goat   _____

Name

Put these words into alphabetical order. They will make a pattern - what is it?

big　　　　　　　　_____

vegetables　　　　_____

come　　　　　　_____

growing　　　　　_____

father　　　　　　_____

daddy　　　　　　_____

sleeping　　　　　_____

at　　　　　　　　_____

tricycles　　　　　_____

wheelbarrow　　　_____

Look at the second letter as well as the first, before putting these words in alphabetical order.

big　　　_____

and　　　_____

but　　　_____

art　　　_____

bat　　　_____

ape　　　_____

Name [ ] [.]

Put a full stop at the end of the sentence.

Look at the sheep ○

Look at the sun ○

Look at the monkey ○

Look at the hammer ○

Look at the motorcycle ○

Look at the frog ○

Look at the ball ○

Look at the fish ○

  Read each sentence.

(Circle) the capital letters only.

(A)a	C c	F f	M m
B b	E e	G g	L l
N n	P p	D d	H h
K k	O o	R r	S s

Name ☐

Put a full stop at the end of the sentence.

Look at the starfish○

Look at the mouse○

Look at the horse○

Look at the hat○

Look at the flower○

Look at the fly○

Look at the bananas○

Look at the baby○

  Read each sentence.

(Circle) the capital letters only.

Q q   T t   W w   Z z

A a   D d   R r   U u

X x   B b   E e   G g

V v   Y y   C c   F f

Name [ ] **S s**

Put in a capital S or a lower case s.

[ ]trawberries are nice to eat.

Look at the [ ]tarfish.

[ ]nakes are animals.

[ ]ocks and shoes.

This is a [ ]hip.

Here is a [ ]heep.

[ ]nails are small.

This is a [ ]hark.

👀 **Read each sentence.**

Circle the words beginning with s.

so
summer
sit
little
it
(sing)
pig
sun
a
some
sea
at
is

Name [ ] **M m**

Put in a capital M or a lower case m.

☐y name is Peter.

This is a ☐ouse.

☐onday is a day of the week.

☐ilk is good to drink.

I love my ☐um.

A ☐oth is like a butterfly.

☐ushrooms are nice to eat.

A ☐onkey is an animal.

👀 **Read each sentence.**

Circle the words beginning with m.

little   look   me   it

an   big   is   mat

mother   mum   my

may   are   a

Name [   ] **H h**

Put in a capital H or a lower case h.

☐ere is a frog.

This is a ☐elicopter.

☐e is a boy.

☐ats go on your head.

A big ☐ouse.

The sun is ☐ot.

☐orses are animals.

Look at the ☐ammer.

👁👁 **Read each sentence.**

Circle the words beginning with h.

to

wing   hat

big   hand   hit

a   hot   had

here   his   he   up

© Curriculum Concepts   Skills for Literacy – Book 1   57

Name [ ] [ ] **F f**

Put in a capital F or a lower case f.

☐ish can swim.

A little ☐rog.

☐lowers smell nice.

☐lies are small.

Here is a ☐ire-engine.

This is a ☐inger

☐ires are hot.

Look at the ☐lag.

👀 **Read each sentence.**

Circle the words beginning with f.

for   fun   and   fit   me

five   small   fat   fish   fun

food   mad   at

Name ☐ **B b**

Put in a capital B or a lower case b.

☐irds are small.

Look at the ☐ell.

☐ananas are yellow.

☐alls are round.

Look at the ☐aby.

Look at the ☐ike.

☐uses are big.

Look at the ☐ear.

👀 **Read each sentence.**

Circle the words beginning with b.

by   bun   band   bat

but   banana   like   be

bit   no   an   look

© Curriculum Concepts — Skills for Literacy – Book 1

Name ☐ **W w**

Put in a capital W or a lower case w.

☐e like school.

Look at the ☐asp.

☐e like watermelon.

☐e like bananas.

Look at the ☐itch.

Look at the ☐heelbarrow.

☐e like playing.

Look at the ☐atch.

👀 **Read each sentence.**

Circle the words beginning with w.

was   we   wet   were

went   good   fit   week   want

wasp   wall   in   apple

Skills for Literacy – Book 1 © Curriculum Concepts

Name ⬜ **P p**

Put in a capital P or a lower case p.

☐irates are bad.

Look at the ☐ig.

My name is ☐eter.

☐ut a hat on.

Look at the ☐encil.

Look at the ☐iano.

☐ies taste good.

Look at the ☐anda.

👀 **Read each sentence.**

Circle the words beginning with p.

pig   pet   pencil   pen   and

pie   here   put   pink

my   pin   it   pan

Name _____ Cc

Put in a capital C or a lower case c.

☐ows make milk.

Look at the ☐ake.

☐lowns are funny.

☐arrots are good to eat.

Look at the ☐ar.

Look at the ☐loud.

☐an you help me?

Look at the ☐at.

👀 **Read each sentence.**

Circle the words beginning with c.

cat   be   sit   big

        bet   go   like

cut   carrot

        can   mat   so